CRAFTS
for kids

Games

Greta Speechley

WAYLAND

This edition published in 2007 by Wayland

Wayland
338 Euston Road
London NW1 3BH

Wayland Australia
Hachette Children's Books
Level 17/207 Kent Street
Sydney, NSW 2000

For The Brown Reference Group plc.
Craftperson: Greta Speechley
Project Editor: Jane Scarsbrook
Designer: Joan Curtis
Photography: Martin Norris
Design Manager: Lynne Ross
Managing Editor: Bridget Giles
Editorial Director: Lindsey Lowe

British Library Cataloguing in Publication Data

Speechley, Greta, 1948-
  Games. - (Crafts for kids)
  1. Handicraft - Juvenile literature 2. Games - Juvenile literature
  I. Title
  745.5'9

ISBN-13: 9780750251594

ISBN: 978-0-7502-5159-4

Printed and bound in Thailand

Wayland is a division of Hachette Children's Books

Contents

Introduction

The projects in this book will keep you busy long after you have finished making them. Try making a solitaire board from salt dough – ours is in the shape of a pizza with olives for counters! You can make a maze from flexible straws, too, and see how quickly your friends can find their way out.

YOU WILL NEED

Each project includes a list of all the things you need. Before you go out and buy lots of new materials, have a look at home to see what you could use instead. For example, you can cut any card shapes out of old boxes. You can find many of the things you need in the store cupboard, such as potatoes, salt dough ingredients, and rice for the juggling balls. You can buy air-drying clay from a craft shop and other items, such as garden sticks and magnets, from a department store.

Getting started

 Read the steps for the project first.

 Gather together all the items you need.

 Cover your work surface with newspaper.

 Wear an apron, or change into old clothes.

A message for adults

All the projects in Games have been designed for children to make, but occasionally they will need you to help. Some of the projects do require the use of sharp items, such as needles and scissors. Please read through the instructions before your child starts work.

Making patterns

Follow these steps to make the patterns on pages 30 and 31. Using a pencil, trace the pattern on to tracing paper. To cut the pattern out of card, turn the tracing over, and lay it on the card. Rub firmly over the pattern with a pencil. The shape will appear on the cardboard. Cut it out. To use a half pattern, trace the shape once, then flip over the tracing paper, and trace again to complete the whole shape. Or follow the instructions for the project.

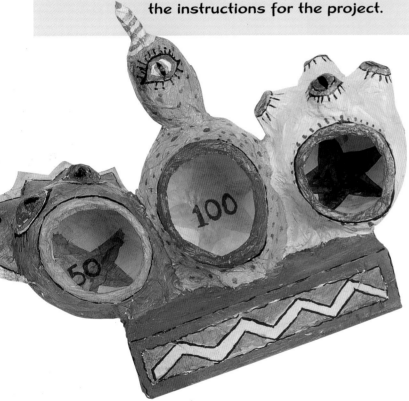

When you have finished

Wash paintbrushes and put everything away.

Put pens, pencils, paints and glue in an old box or ice cream container.

Keep scissors and other sharp items in a safe place.

Stick needles and pins into a pincushion or a piece of scrap cloth.

BE SAFE

Look out for the safety boxes. They will appear whenever you need to ask an adult for help.

Ask an adult to help you use sharp scissors.

Bee football

This is a fun version of table football with buzzing bee strikers. Why not make a stadium from a bigger box, and add more bee players for a 5-a-side match.

YOU WILL NEED

large cereal box	green felt for the field
pencil	coloured felt for the bees
felt-tip pens	glitter pens
scissors	net fruit bag
white paper	glue
two wooden skewers	ping-pong ball
hole punch	tape

1 Cut off one large side of a cereal box to make the sports stadium. Now cut out a square at either end to make two goals, leaving a bar of card across the top of each. Tape a piece of netting from a fruit bag over each to make two goal nets.

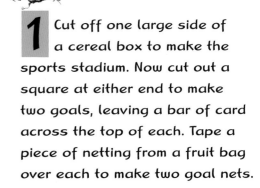

2 Cut pieces of paper the same length as each side of the stadium and at least twice as high. Fold each strip in half so that they fit over the side walls. Cut out spaces for the goals – draw around the pieces you cut out from the box to get the size right. Draw and colour in the crowd, with their faces on one side and their backs on the other. Place the paper over the walls, and tape them down.

6

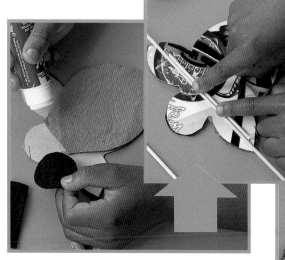

3 Cut a piece of green felt the same size as the base of the box, and glue it inside.

4 To make a bee player, cut two bee shapes the same shape and size out of card or a cereal box. Decorate each piece with felt in a team colour. Glue wooden skewers to the back of one piece, and then glue the other on top. Make a second bee wearing different team colours.

5 Draw on the players' numbers, and decorate their wings using a glitter pen.

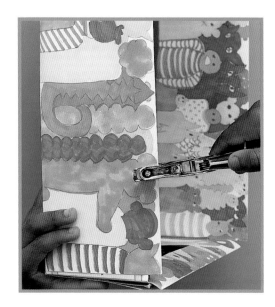

6 Punch two sets of holes in the walls of the stadium for the wooden skewers to fit through. Position the holes so that the bees swing without hitting the floor and do not hit the wall when you swing them back for a kick. Now put a ping-pong ball in the centre of the field and blow the whistle for kick-off.

Butterfly racers

Try out different types of string and thread to see which lets your butterfly race fastest. A really smooth, shiny piece of string tied tightly should do the best job.

YOU WILL NEED

white card	tracing paper
felt-tip pens	pencil
straws	pipe cleaners
scissors	needle
smooth string	
glue	

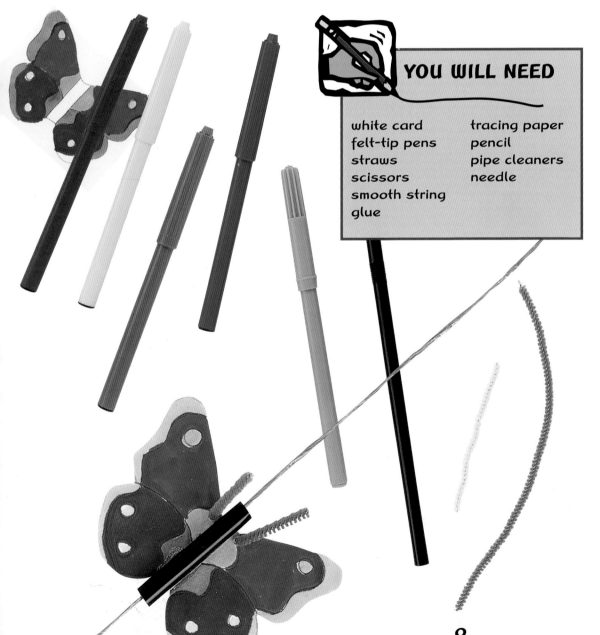

1 Trace the butterfly on page 31. Turn the tracing over on to a piece of white card. Rub over the lines with your pencil. The butterfly will appear on the card. Go over the lines to make them stand out more.

2 Colour in the butterfly with felt-tip pens. Remember, butterflies have symmetrical patterns, so colour in both wings the same way.

8

3 Cut a short piece of straw and glue it along the middle of the butterfly.

Ask an adult to help you make holes for the antennae.

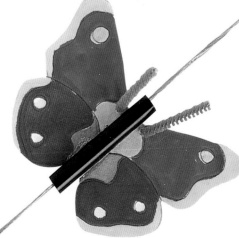

4 Make two holes for the antennae using a needle. Push a short piece of pipe cleaner through – each end sticking through to make one antenna.

5 Thread each butterfly on to a piece of smooth string. Tie the strings up at an angle, for example, from the top of a table leg to the bottom of a chair leg. When you have a few butterfly tracks set up, hold the butterflies at the top and then let them fly!

9

Roller ball

Hit the jackpot by rolling a marble through the middle door for 100 points. Take turns with a friend and keep score as you go.

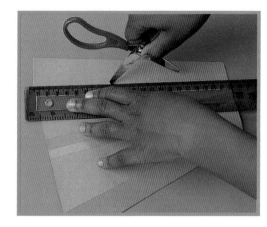

1 To make the ramp for the marble to roll down, first trace the pattern on page 30. It is a half pattern, so trace it once, flip over the tracing paper, and trace again – using the centre line as a guide. Transfer the tracing on to orange card by following the instructions on page 5. Cut the shape out. Score along the fold lines using scissors and a ruler. Ask an adult to help you.

2 Fold along the scored lines as shown to make the ramp. Tape the two end pieces together underneath.

10

Ask an adult to help you score along the folds in the ramp.

3 To make the scoreboard, cut a foam pizza base in half. Cut out two slits at either end – the slits should be the same width as the foam and 2 cm (³⁄₄ in) long.

4 To make the stands, cut out two triangles with wide bases from the leftover foam. Cut slits in the top points to match the slits in the scoreboard. Now cut out five v-shapes along the flat bottom of the scoreboard. Make the middle one the tallest.

5 Decorate the scoreboard with poster paints. We have stuck on some starry gift-wrap ribbon, too. Above the v-shape holes paint on the scores: 5, 10, 20, 50, and 100 points for the middle hole.

6 Let the paint dry and then fit the stands into the scoreboard. Now set up your ramp, and try to roll a marble through the holes in the scoreboard.

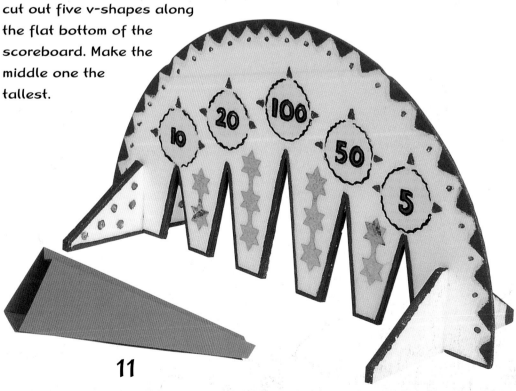

Noughts and crosses

Collect the smoothest, roundest pebbles you can find to make a garden game of noughts and crosses. The board is made from sticks that are used to help plants grow straight.

YOU WILL NEED

eight pebbles	paintbrush
four garden	varnish
sticks	scissors
red twine	black marker
or string	pen
poster paints	

1 Wash the pebbles and let them dry completely. Paint a pale-blue circle on to four pebbles. We have mixed blue paint with white to make pastel blue. Let the paint dry.

2 Paint a red cross on to the four blue pebbles, and dot around the edge of the blue circle with green paint. Let the paint dry and varnish the pebbles.

3 Paint a yellow circle on each of the other four pebbles. Dot around the edge of the circles with red paint. Let the paint dry. Draw an "0" on to each pebble using a black marker pen. Varnish the pebbles.

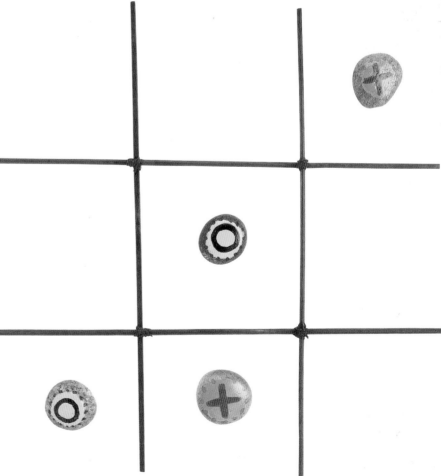

4 Lay two garden sticks down and place two on top across them. Tie them at the joints with red twine. Now challenge someone to a game – first to get three 0s or Xs in a row is the winner!

Monster mouths

You can aim and fire a ping-pong ball across the room with this balloon shooter. Set aside a couple of days to make the monster mouth goals – the papier mâché needs to dry overnight.

YOU WILL NEED

large cereal box
three round balloons and one thin balloon
egg crate
poster paints
cardboard
tape

black marker pen
tissue paper
paintbrush
toilet roll tube
PVA glue
scissors
sponge
string

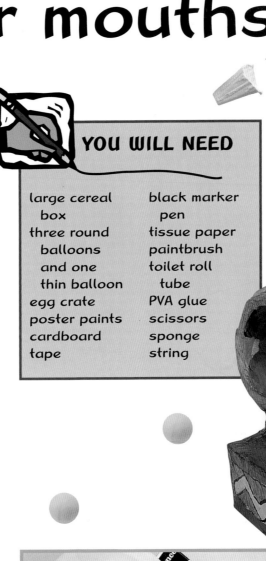

1 Blow up three balloons, tie knots in the necks, and tape them on top of a large cereal box.

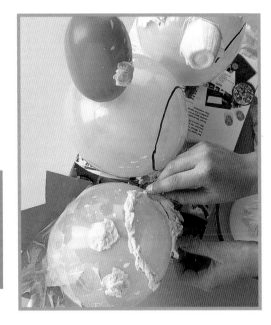

2 To make each monster an individual, tape eyes cut out from an egg crate on to one. Blow up a long, thin balloon, leaving a waggly tip, and tape it onto the middle balloon. Finally, cut out a card crest and tape it on to the third balloon. Draw a big mouth on to the front of each monster face with a marker pen.

3 Mix up half PVA glue and half water. Tear strips of tissue paper, dip them into the paste, and scrunch them up to make eyes and lips for the monsters. Paste them on. Now cover the whole goal, except for the mouths, with a layer of tissue paper. Paste on two more layers. Let the goal dry overnight in a warm, dry place. When it is dry, pop the balloons and paint the goals, adding a score inside each mouth.

4 To make the shooter, paint a toilet roll tube in bright colours. To decorate, cut out a star-shaped hole from scrap paper. Cut out a piece of sponge, dip it in the paint and dab it over the stencil to make a neat star.

5 Cut a hole in the round end of a balloon. Tie a knot in the neck and tie a piece of wool or string around the knot. Now dangle the string through the tube, and stretch the balloon over the end. Push a ping-pong ball into the balloon, and pull back the string at the back. Let it go to make the ball shoot out and into a monster mouth!

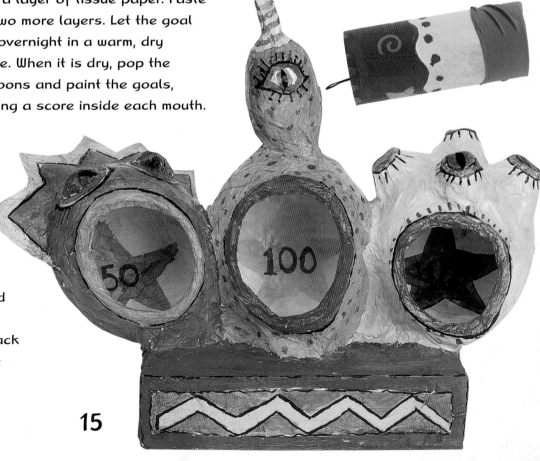

Potato bugs

To play this game, first spin the spinner. If it lands on a bug leg, then stick one leg into your potato. Now it's the next player's turn. Keep playing until one of you has built a bug.

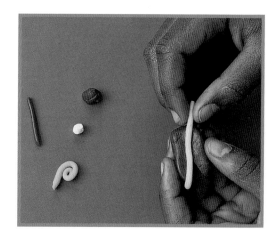

YOU WILL NEED

air-drying clay (hardens in the oven)
toothpicks
scissors
baking tray
small biscuit cutter

clay cutter
small potatoes
white card
pencil
felt-tip pens
compass
ruler

1 For each bug make a head, a crest, a spine, six legs and a tail. Make a different-coloured bug for each player. Shape a head for the red bug from clay and cut a v-shape out for the mouth. Roll a thin sausage of yellow clay to line the mouth and make a thin spiral tongue from green clay. Press the pieces on to the head and press on two clay eyes.

2 To make the crest above the bug's head, roll out red clay with a round pencil and press out a piece using a small biscuit cutter. Cut out a v-shape from the crest that will fit over the bug's head. Decorate the crest with yellow and blue clay.

16

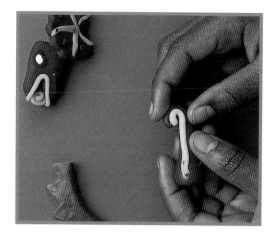

3 To make the tail, roll a thick sausage of red clay between your palms so that one end is thinner. Press a strip of yellow clay on to one side and roll up the tip of the tail. Cut out a zigzag spine from flattened red clay.

4 Make six bug legs from red clay. Add a blue foot at one end. Cut the ends off toothpicks. Push a toothpick end into each bug body part so you can stick them into the potato. Bake the pieces following the instructions on the clay package. Ask an adult to help you.

5 To make the spinner, draw a circle onto white card using a compass. Place the point of the compass on the edge of the circle. Make two marks where the pencil crosses the circle edge. Put the compass point on one of these marks and make another mark in the same way. Go on until you have six marks. Join each mark to the next with a ruled line to make a hexagon. Rule lines between opposite points on the hexagon to divide it into six triangles.

Ask an adult to help you bake the clay pieces.

6 Draw a bug body part on to each triangle. Leave one triangle blank. Push a toothpick into the centre of the spinner and begin the game.

Balloon jugglers

This project takes five minutes tops, but learning to juggle takes weeks! First practise juggling two balls in one hand. When you can do that with your right hand and your left hand, three balls will be easy.

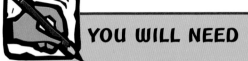

YOU WILL NEED

six balloons in different colours	bowl rice scissors

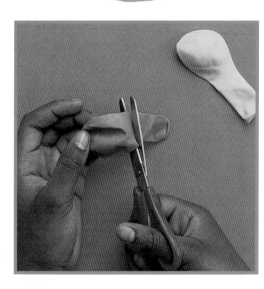

1 To make one ball, first choose two balloons in contrasting colours. To stretch them a little, blow them up and hold for 30 seconds before you let the air out. Cut the necks off the balloons.

18

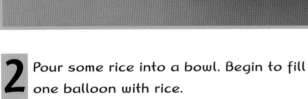
2 Pour some rice into a bowl. Begin to fill one balloon with rice.

3 As you push in more rice, the balloon will stretch and get bigger. Keep pushing in rice until the ball is a comfortable size to fit in your hand.

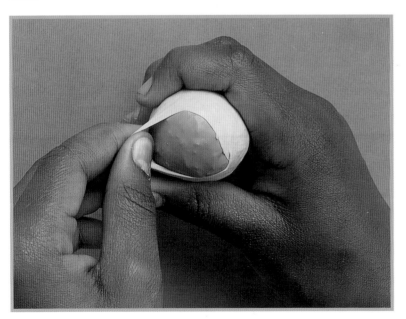

4 Stretch the second balloon over the first to hold in the rice. Make two more juggling balls in the same way but in different, bright colours.

19

Pizza solitaire

Set up the pizza solitaire board with the middle hole empty. Move any counter by jumping over its neighbour and taking away that counter. Keep going – the aim is to end up with just one counter in the centre.

YOU WILL NEED

To make the salt dough:	rolling pin
2 cups of plain flour	clay cutter
	kitchen foil
1 cup of salt	baking tray
1 cup of lukewarm water mixed with a tablespoon of cooking oil	white paper
	pencil
	toothpick
	scissors
	small plate
	small marble
	poster paints
	paintbrush
extra flour for rolling	varnish

1 Mix up the salt dough ingredients in a bowl. Knead the dough until it doesn't feel sticky anymore. Sprinkle the kitchen surface with flour and roll out the dough. Cut a circular board out of the dough – cut around a plate if it helps.

3 Take off the paper and use the edge of a saucer to make a groove along the inner circle. Press a small marble into the toothpick pricks to make dents.

4 Roll 32 round counters from dough – they should fit in the dents on the pizza. Put them on a separate, lined baking tray. Ask an adult to bake the board and the counters in the oven at 110°C (230°F; Gas Mark ¼) for 30 minutes. Let it cool. Roll the counters in a saucer of watered-down black paint so that they look like olives.

2 Line a baking tray with foil and lay the dough inside. Cut out a circle of white paper the same size as the pizza. Draw a circle 1 cm (½ in) from the edge and a pattern of dots like the one above. Lay the paper on to the dough and prick through the dots and along the circle with a toothpick. Cut out mushrooms, tiny fish and salami shapes from the leftover dough and press them on to the pizza.

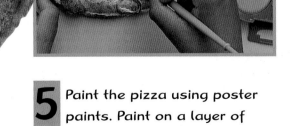

5 Paint the pizza using poster paints. Paint on a layer of varnish to finish off.

Ask an adult to bake the salt dough.

Balloon catcher

Blow up the balloon to just the right size to fit snugly in the pot. It will make the game especially tricky.

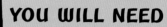

YOU WILL NEED

yellow tissue paper	yarn
blue paper	thick string
PVA glue	clear glue
small balloon	scissors
large green plastic drink bottle	glitter pens
	paintbrush
	mixing bowl
	thin tinsel

1 Cut the top off a plastic drink bottle. It will be the catching pot. Glue a piece of thick string around the pot in a spiral from the bottle top to the rim.

2 Cut out triangles of blue paper and glue them around the spiral, as shown, to make a pretty pattern.

3 Mix up half PVA glue and water in a bowl. Tear yellow tissue paper into strips and paste them on to the pot over the string and blue paper triangles. One layer is enough. Let it dry.

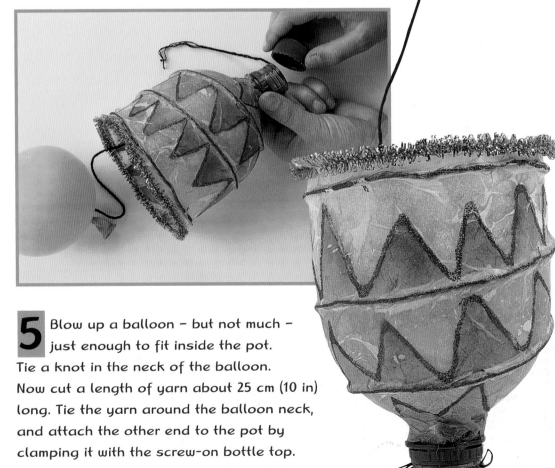

4 Go over the string spiral and the triangles with a glitter pen. To add a final touch, glue thin tinsel around the rim of the pot.

5 Blow up a balloon – but not much – just enough to fit inside the pot. Tie a knot in the neck of the balloon. Now cut a length of yarn about 25 cm (10 in) long. Tie the yarn around the balloon neck, and attach the other end to the pot by clamping it with the screw-on bottle top.

Draughts

Draughts is one of the oldest games in the world. Make your own board and counters and teach a friend to play. You could make a set of chess pieces for your board, too – a draughts board and a chess board are exactly the same.

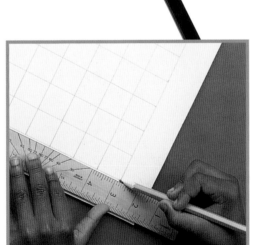

1 To make the board, cut a square 25 cm x 25 cm (10 in x 10 in) from white cardboard. Rule a border 2.5 cm (1 in) wide. Make marks every 2.5 cm (1 in) along each side of the centre square. Join them up to make a grid of 64 squares.

2 Cut two squares of sponge the same size as the squares of the board. Mix up two colours of paint. We have used orange and pale blue. Stamp the squares alternate colours – orange, blue, orange, blue and so on. Paint the border a different colour.

3 Draw a big star and a small star on to scrap paper and cut out the star-shaped holes to make stencils. Use a sponge stamp to stencil a dark-blue star on each pale-blue square. Stencil a big star into the four corners of the board.

HOW TO PLAY

1. In draughts you only play on the orange squares. To start, both players place eight counters on the orange squares in the first two rows nearest them.

2. Take turns moving a piece forward diagonally one square.

3. If the square on the diagonal left or right is occupied by your opponent's counter and there is an empty square on the diagonal line after it, jump over the counter and capture it. Put it to one side.

4. You can make a series of jumps if you land and then there is another opportunity to jump.

5. If you reach the opposite side of the board, crown your piece with one of the spare counters. Now you can move backwards as well as forwards – but still only diagonally one square.

6. You win when you have captured all your opponent's counters.

4 To make the counters, mix up the salt dough ingredients in a bowl. Knead the dough until it doesn't feel sticky. Sprinkle flour on to the kitchen surface and the dough. Roll out the dough, and cut out 24 small counters using a bottle top. Put the counters onto a baking tray lined with baking paper. Cover them with kitchen foil to keep them from burning. Ask an adult to cook them in the oven at 110°C (230°F) for about 30 minutes. Let them cool. Now paint them. Stencil a star on to 12 counters and a heart on to the other 12 counters.

Fish for treasure

Dip a fishing rod into the treasure chest and see what you catch. This is a game that a younger brother or sister will love to play with you.

1 To turn a small box into a wooden treasure chest, first paint the outside brown. When the paint has dried, draw on lines and swirls with a thin black felt-tip pen to look like wooden planks. Cut out corners and a lock for the chest from gold paper and glue them on.

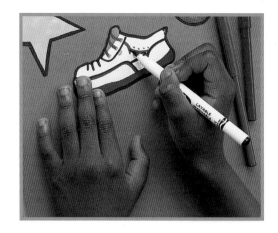

2 Line the box with pieces of kitchen foil. Glue chocolate coin wrappers or foil bottle tops around the inside edge to look like shiny coins.

3 Draw bolts on to the gold corners and a keyhole on to the lock using a black felt-tip pen. To make the chest look as if it has been sitting on the seabed for centuries, splatter different coloured paints all over using a toothbrush.

4 Think up lots of things that you might catch on a fishing rod. There are some patterns for you to trace on pages 30 and 31. Transfer the patterns on to white card by following the instructions on page 5. Cut out the card shapes and colour them in. Write the number of points you score for catching each one on the back.

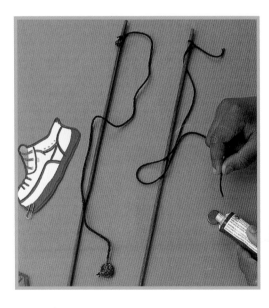

5 To make a fishing rod, tie a length of string to the end of a garden stick. Glue a small magnet to the other end of the string. Make a second rod for the other player. Push paper clips onto the pieces of card so you can pick them up with the magnet.

Marble maze

The paths in this maze are made from flexible straws. The bends make perfect corners for the marble to roll around. Trace our maze, or work out one of your own.

YOU WILL NEED

flexible straws	smooth white
net from fruit	mounting
bag	board
scissors	ruler
clear glue	tracing paper
marble	scrap paper
blue poster	pencil
paint	marble
paintbrush	

1 Trace the maze on page 31. Use a ruler to draw the straight lines. Transfer the tracing on to smooth, white board by following the instructions on page 5. Cut out the maze and cut out a square at the cross. Ask an adult to cut the board with a craft knife for a smooth edge.

Ask an adult to cut the mounting board with a craft knife to get a smooth edge.

28

2 Cut flexible straws to cover the lines of the maze. Use the bend in the straw for the corners. When you have cut a piece to the correct length, draw a trail of clear glue along the line and press on the straw. When you have finished, let the glue dry.

3 Paint on a star to show where the starting point on your maze is. This is where you put the marble to begin.

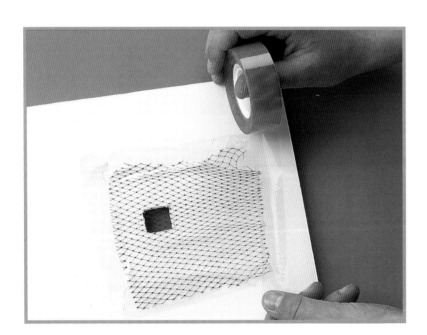

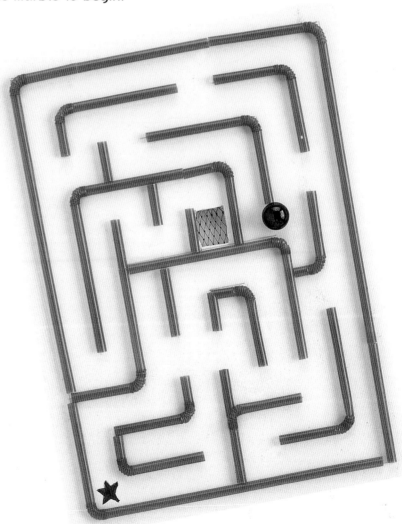

4 Tape a piece of netting from a fruit bag on to the back of the maze under the finishing hole. It will catch the marble.

Patterns

Here are the patterns you will need to make some of the projects. To find out how to make a pattern, follow the instructions in the "Making patterns" box on page 5. Some of the patterns are half patterns. There are instructions to help you use the half patterns in the steps for the project.

Fish for treasure page 26

Fish for treasure page 26

Fish for treasure page 26

Roller ball page 10 (half pattern)

centre line – line up this edge when making template

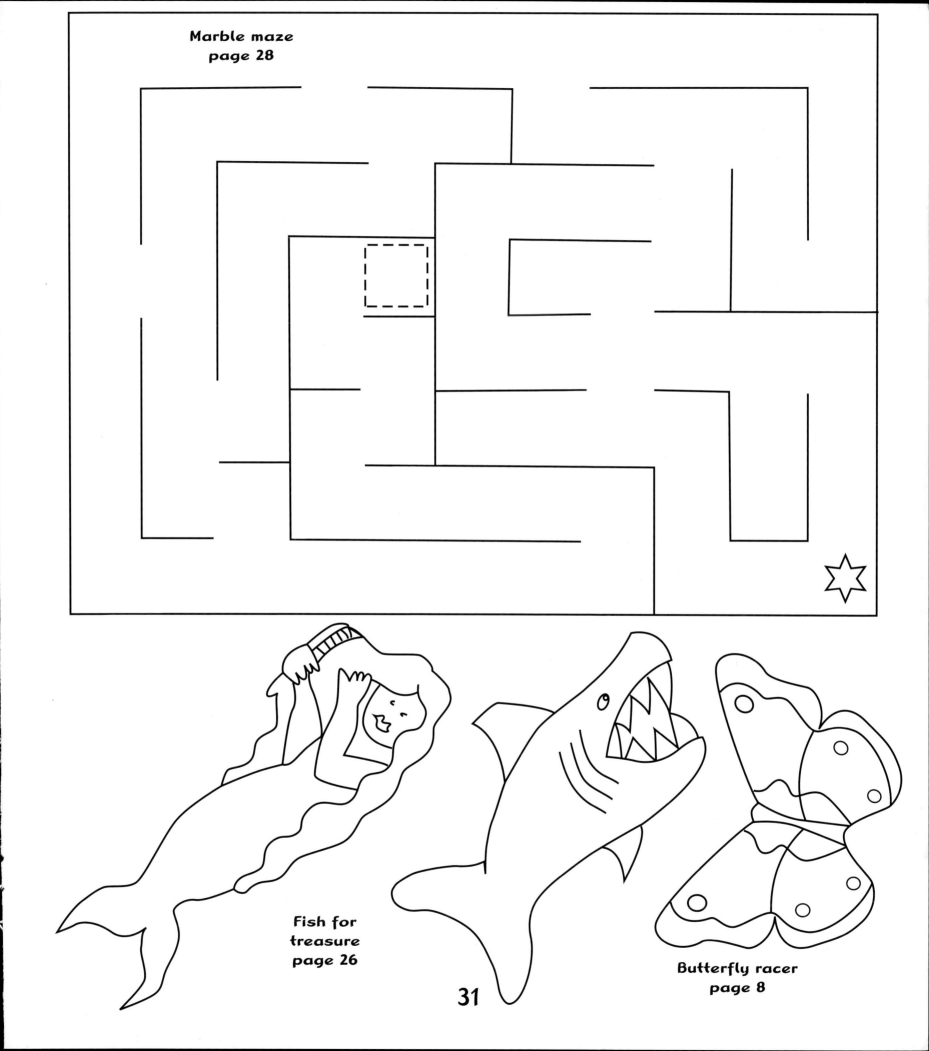

Marble maze
page 28

Fish for
treasure
page 26

Butterfly racer
page 8

31

Index